'HARKHEINDZEL' KENNY OMIYALE

Intelligent
Personal Branding

The future of your brand

DEDICATION

To every Creative out there who believe in their brands, who are passionate about their message and who are confident that their vision would reach the ends of the earth.

KEEP BELIEVEING IN YOURSELF!

CONTENT

INTRODUCTION

We live in a world of great change. The **Post Covid-19** era has disrupted man of the systems, structures, strategies and curricula that we have founded our brands and businesses upon. And to this end, there needs to be a swift revision about our personal growth models and personal branding strategies.

Not everything you have learnt in the past decade is useless. So, in this book, I would seek to bring to light some of the things you should hold on to, some of the things to throw away and many of the things you need to learn in order to be relevant and become the preference brand in the new era.

Go through this book with an open mind. I would be as pragmatic as I can, but really, the most of the job would be yours to apply.

Your brand is important. Brands are evolving as culture and technology evolves. I am sure you know that the age of technology has evolved, therefore culture is making the necessary adjustments and to this end, you brand must also make that shift.

I wish you the very best as you take this journey.

Cheers,

'Harkheindzel' Kenny Omiyale
The Spiritumentalyst

INTELLIGENT PERSONAL BRANDING
The future of your brand.

Branding is about modelling, communication, perception and executions. And to do this effectively, you need to be versed in the skill of plotting and engaging future trends. You must understand how to plot trends based on political, social, cultural and technological inclinations of humans.

In the new age of technology, you must learn the process of work effectiveness which is found no longer in delegation but in **automation**.
This is the goal of businesses in the new age. *How can I make sure that the basic things I do in my business are automated?* This will allow you to think of other ways of growing and improving your brand. This doesn't keep you occupied with basic operational tasks but you will only serve in supervisory, feedback and management control roles just to make sure that things are going the way they ought to go.

This is where AI (Artificial Intelligence) comes in. For your brand to be intelligent, it must be able to make working easier for you while it presents you with the potential to increase the scope of your brand and business.

This allows you to get properties in the more important space of the technology era which is known as DIGITAL SOCIAL SPACE.

Social capital is going to be one of the hugest blessings for a successful brand in the post 2020 era. This is why as an intelligent brand; you must begin to work on forging your own community around your brand message and ideology.

It is no longer news that our world has changed. Our realities and hence, perceptions have evolved. This is obvious in the trajectory of the economy, commerce, social relationships an altogether life expectation

Let me take you through a brief simple history of communication from the 1990s.

There was a time that the only means of communication was through typewriter. That was how memos were created and sent across the world. So, we had the typewriters and the papers which were the major means of communication, but as we moved towards the Year 2000, we evolved into the internet age. Let's call this the age of internet 1.0

From 2000-2009, there and about, it was the first experience into the global digital age. As papers evolved, it began to reduce in official use. We had what was known as the electronic mail (e-mail) which was an easier, faster and more efficient way of communication

In the years 2000-2019, we entered the age of internet 2.0. In this age, we experienced better speed of transfer, data and connectivity where there were phases of development from 2G to 4G connection speed.

From 2020-2029, we have the age of internet 3.0 which I would call *metanet*. In this age, due to the great speed of connection (and the proposition of the 5th generation of internet speed 5G). we will be able to venture into a new world of limitless perceptions and realities. It is from this point that AI (Artificial Intelligence) evolves into AC (Artificial Consciousness). At this point, VR (Virtual Reality) will become habitable meaning people would be able to spend more time online in a virtual reality where they would be able to do almost anything that could be done on land viz; home, food, clothing, social life, work, etc. Just imagine it and it would be possible.

At that point, paper will be so reduced that it would affect currency. This would be the introduction to digital currency. With this change, banking will evolve as commercial transactions will adapt to the new technology

So here is my question to you.

With all I just mentioned to you, would you think your products right now would still be relevant in this new age?

Here are a few things that you need to change or be mindful of if you want to stay profitable in business in the new age.
- *Brand communication*
- *Brand security*
- *Brand economy or commerce.*
- *Brand perception.*

SCOPE OF INTELLIGENT PERSONAL BRANDING
YOU MUST EMBRACE AND MASTER

Brand product,
Brand perception,
Brank market,
Brand story.

BRAND PRODUCT:
A product is that which gives you the authority or right to engage a market. The market has become a complex system of cascading data, cacophony and persuasion power tussles that if you do not know how to plan your point of entry as a brand, you will be swallowed up in the cyber-noise and traffic of data.

Therefore, in the market, there is a rule. It is known as the rule of trade and this rule states that;

"You do not have a sustained right to stay in (any) market if you do not have a commodity to trade or exchange."

What this means is that for you to get any attention in any market, *you must either be solving a problem or providing a solution or both.*

This means that your product or service must be the subset of your brand if you want to get any attention in the market.

HSI COMPLETE PRODUCT CYCLE:

Here at Harkheindzel School of Innovation, we have designed a product cycle that any intelligent brand must learn and master in order to remain in charge of your business systems and operational structures.

This cycle starts from the point of ideation to the point of reaching and engaging with your market.

Below are the 10 step cycles of the HSI complete product cycle.

1. **Ideation:** *from mind to head.*
In the process of designing a product, you must not fall prey of an illusion of prowess that many creatives fall for. It is known as *the idea of your idea*. When an idea is in your mind, it usually looks foolproof and bound to succeed, but this is because you have the creators bias which is a state of mind where a creator believes that because he designed a product, then it is bound to succeed (because he is either knowledgeable or passionate about his product).

In this first phase, you must bring your idea from your mind to your head. This is the point where in your mind you have mind-stormed the various issues that may arise in the product formulation and design. When it gets to your head, the design is already taking a shape and having a form howbeit in your head.

2. **Needs Analysis:** *mind to market mind.*
After you have gotten the product in your head, you must now begin to test it with the market trends or

reality that you are aware of. All of these would still be taking place in your head. You must be able to answer as many questions as you can ask about the power, persuasion and perception of your product.

Questions like;
- *What is this product really about?*
- *Why am I creating this product?*
- *What are the 5 qualities or factors that will ensure the success of this product?*
- *Who are the people that this product is designed to help?*
- *What are 5 basic challenges I could face in the design of this product?*
- *What is the relevant timeline for this product? Would it still be relevant in the next 5years?*

Etc.

3. **Product Power**: *(Idealistic) satisfaction with producer. (on paper)*

This is the point you need to write all the questions you have asked yourself and the answers you have provided on paper. The point you put your thoughts on paper is the first time your idea begins to take a physical form because you have done the first thing in bringing ideas to life which is to capture the idea on paper.

4. **Product formation**: *from paper to reality (substance)*

This is the phase when you begin to give your idea a physical form. If your idea is a book, this is the time you begin to write the first chapter of the book. If it is an app, this is when you begin to write the code and design the graphics and structure. Whatever the case is, this is the point where you have something tangible and visible that represents a part of the product you are designing or creating. The smallest physical representation of your product is better than the strongest mental idea that you have because things are stronger when they have a physical influence or tangible representation.

5. **Reliability or relevance**: *testing with market reality.*

You must have heard of **beta testing** of products. This is the point you are testing the product for bugs, for defects or quality control. If it is a book, this is the time you send it to an editor to proofread and edit it. If it is an app, this is the time you open it up for beta testing where people use it and test it to see if it works according to its intended design.

This is an important phase because you need the feedback to fine-tune your product so that it would serve its intended purpose by the time you release it to the market.

6. **Product awareness**: *initiate product into market.*

It is a strategic point of action to build the awareness of your product before it hits the market. Awareness is a powerful thing in perception. Awareness is what introduces your product to the market. It is the first time the market gets to know about the existence of your product.

If the product is a book, this is the time you make pre-order copies available or you have free bonus chapters for people to read. If it is an app, this is the time you make advertisements to bring the knowledge of your product to the market or you have demo versions for download. At this point, you need to do all you can to make sure that you have a strong brand message and the message is very attention grabbing and persuasive.

7. **Product communication**: *engage the product to market space.*

This is the point you engage every initiative and persuasive means to maintain product clarity. You must own your narrative. When communicating your product to the market, you must make sure that you answer any probable questions you foresee the market is going to ask about the relevance, benefit and value your product would provide.

Do not give room for misinterpretation, do your due diligence to learn the language of the market and use this language to communicate with the market.

Many brands miss the point here when they begin to speak intellectual jargons and high-sounding words, the market is not interested in all of that. You need to communicate in plain clear terms that would be clear and simple and straight to the point. Do not beat about the bush. Speak to the market, engage their minds and emotions. Be sure that your language ignites their desire, attention and attraction towards the value of the product.

"Focus on the value and not just the price"

8. **Product interaction/experience**: *market contact and engage with product.*

Here is the first time the market gets to experience your product. It is at this point that your integrity resounds. Always over deliver when it comes to your brand promise. This is the point you score emotional points with the market. If your product is loved, you would begin to get good feedback and referrals. One of the best ways to ensure your brand grows is when you get loyal customers who become your free marketers and ambassadors.

9. **Product stability:** *market assessment of your product.*

You must continue to engage the market from this point. At this point, you must add some form of mental engagements to your branding approach. There are many brands that have a good launching but months down the line, they end up becoming bankrupt because many do not realize that launching is not the proof of a successful brand but the sustainability of the brand. A brand is sustained when you realize that social capital is one of the needed modern cash-flow that is needed for any brand to thrive. You must make sure that people keep thinking about your brand.

One of the ways to do this is to always make sure that there is something news-worthy about your brand. Always find new ways to engage the market, talk about the things that matter to them, build a community around your brand message and ideology. Have paraphernalia that would multiply the awareness of your brand and more important than all would be to have excellent products and superb marketing and top-notch customer and client services.

10. Product feedback and review: *adaptation and evolution of product.*

On the path to brand growth, there comes a time you will need the market, most especially your loyal clients to do part of the thinking for you. This is the point you ask for feedback from your users, clients or customers. Getting feedback can be directly or indirectly. Either ways, get feedback and use them to adapt your product and services towards the needs and desires of your market. As must as this be necessary, you do not have to go all out to go with everything the market wants. Be sure that the feedback is in line with your strategic goals.

Major feedback can be done in the area of client satisfaction and emotional appeal and delivery but for those who have tangible products, you will learn to balance it with your company objectives and other measures you operate with.

If your product hasn't gone through these steps, it's far from being intelligent.

PRODUCTS:

Products can be tangible or intangible. These can be in the form of AI solutions, digital form, apps, books, consumables, persons, services.

The experience of products can be; spiritual, emotional, intellectual (or ideological), social (groups and communities), etc.

In this new age and time, you can't be satisfied with one or two scopes of products. You need to combine as many scopes as your product can have to make sure that all the needs of the market are being engaged.

To ponder:
How many of the words (scopes and experiences) above currently qualify your product?
How many others do you think will increase the product power of your brand?

....
....
....
....
....
....
....
....

BRAND PERSONALITY

A brand without a personality is difficult to engage with or remember.

From an objective view (without producer's sentimental bias), mention 3 words that best describe the experience of your brand.

....

....

....

....

Better still, what are the words that your clients have used to describe your product or brand in the past? (whether positive or negative words)

....

....

....

....

Who are the kinds of people who constantly or frequently patronize your brand?

....

....

....

The personality of a brand is something that draws certain kind of people to your brand. Which is also part of your brand perception.

You may think your brand is premium, but if cheap people keep seeking you out, then it means your brand perception is cheap. DEAL WITH IT!

If you sell product and people usually try to over-negotiate the price or people tend to get your product on credit then you do not have a premium brand perception. You may think you do but when it comes to market perception and reality, you don't.

The market is a major determinant of the nature and perception of your brand. But you must also do your job by influencing the kind of narrative you want for your brand.

There is a way you see your product and there is a way the market sees it. Many times, they are not the same unless you have done a good job at being intentional and deliberate on your brand story and the way you conduct the business of your brand.

BRAND - MARKET RATIO PERCEPTION
The total perception of your brand is 30% how you see it and 60% how the market perceives it.

Did you notice there's a missing 10%?

Right!

The 10% is your persuasion power or reconstruction system to emphasize or communicate your intended brand personality.

So, if you think the market isn't getting the core message of your brand, you have 10% to work with to change their mind.

How does this work;

This works through persistence, education or information, if you stick to the brand personality and perception you really want, one of two things would happen;

1. You re-educate part of your clients and they adapt.
2. They are unable to come to terms with the message or your new explanations of it so they leave your brand. (Meaning you can lose clients if what you are trying to re-educate them with is too far from what they already perceive your brand product as)

BRAND PERSONALITY SPECTRUM

Your brand personality can fall within the following:

1. **Authority**: When your brand is focused on a strong message of *domination, expertise, excellence, or premium culture and experience.*

2. **Creative**: When your brand is *dynamic, mobile, flexible, innovative, upward veering, thoughtful and detailed and aesthetic.*

3. **Social**: When your brand is specific about *building interest groups, connecting like-minded or people of similar inclinations, youthful energy and excitement, community action and development.*

4. **Structure**: When your brand ideology is centered *around order, rules and agreement to structures and system focused.*

SO, WHAT IS YOUR BRAND PERSONALITY?

....

Remember, your brand personality determines the kind of people you attract and keep

It takes work to maintain a brand personality. But when it sticks to the market and clients, the brand begins to sell itself.

YOUR BRAND PERSONALITY MAY NOT BE ANYTHING LIKE YOU

Your brand personality can sometimes be different from you as a person. E.g. your brand may have a different contact detail from your personal details or you may create a system for a well-structured dominating brand while your personal attributes can be youthful and playful. etc.

ELEMENTS OF BRAND PERCEPTION:
Brand perception engages the sense and communicates with the senses and the mind of people.

To this end, brand perceptions can have the following elements:

Visual: What you look like,
Audio: How you sound like or talk like.
Emotional: The feelings and aura of your brand
Experience: The mental taste of your brand.
Positioning: As a brand, are you the go-to expert in your industry?

NEUROLINGUISTIC PROGRAMMING AND BRAND PERCEPTION.

'Neurolinguistic' is just one big word that means there are certain words that hold different brain power compared to others and there are certain patterns to use them to get the best of words.

There are certain words or sounds or languages that trigger certain actions in the human brain

Especially when we are in a digital age where you will not always be present to tell people what you mean with the words they hear. You must go the extra mile to make sure you speak the language that their brain understands.

When you want to engage a digital audience or client, first you need their **attention**, then you need to get their **action** (which can include clicking a status or taking specific action)

To do this well, you need to master Sensory Modality and Participant Verbatims (SMPV)

As a customer facing brand representative, if you ask a customer about buying a new car and you see her eyes go up, you might ask what she looks for because her eyes going up revealed that she was seeing pictures in her mind. Similarly, if you ask a person about buying a new car and you see her eyes go horizontally, you might ask what she listens for, because her eyes going sideways revealed that she was hearing words or sounds in her mind.

Again, you need to test your assumptions. Left-handed people often have reversed eye movements from the general population. Some people move their entire head instead of moving their eyes. Important note: Someone leaning back with his eyes staring at the ceiling may simply be accessing the visual part of his mind. You can test whether he is tracking with you by asking, "What do you see?" If his head shakes before he answers, he was probably daydreaming; however, if he keeps staring as he talks you through what he is seeing, chances are he needs to look up to fully access his ability to visualize. When you speak into a participant's primary modality, you make it easier for that person to share what's inside his or her head. Sometimes, the results can look remarkable. People reveal themselves in ways they normally would not.

(Courtesy Branding Strategy Insider)

Notes

....

....

....

....

....

....

....

....

....

....

....

SENSORY MODALITY AND PARTICIPANT VERBATIMS

Sensory modalities are part of a Neurolinguistic programming (NLP) model that identifies patterns in how people externalize the information they are processing. When participants talk, they often speak from a state of mind that is more closely aligned with one sense over another. For instance:

Visual sense:
That's a bright idea. I see how I can use the car's extra space.

Auditory sense:
I hear how this makes sense. Let me tell you — this is a winner.

Kinesthetic sense:
How fast can I accelerate? I feel like this car was made for me.

Olfactory sense:
Smells like a winner. Some ideas stink, but this is coming up roses.

Gustatory sense:
That new car looks yummy. It has the fine flavour of elegance.

When you hear someone speak in a particular sensory modality, and you ask questions in that same modality, the person is more likely to continue talking than if you ask a question in a different sensory modality. You are also more likely to get a congruent answer and more likely to keep the participant engaged.

We can see inside the customers' minds — and know how they are processing information or which parts of their brain they are accessing — by their eye movement. Have you ever noticed how a person's eyes move when you ask them a question? Try this sometime soon. Ask someone this series of questions:

What did it look like the last time it rained?

What are the lyrics to "We are the world"?

Then, watch the person's eyes. their eyes will most likely go the same direction each time, because both questions solicit a recollection. Chances are good that the eyes will go to the right (the person's left) after each question because approximately 85% of the Western world's population that has been tested accesses memories by looking to their left. If you want to see a more subtle distinction, when you ask someone to recollect a visual, the person will likely look up and to your right. If you ask someone to recollect a sound, however, the person will likely look directly to your right (their left) along a horizontal plane

PACING AND LEADING

"Pacing and Leading" in NLP. This starts by subtly mirroring a client's physical expression as a way of creating rapport. Think about how a baby delights in being copied. On some level, we all feel "seen" and understood when another person gestures the way we do or uses the same speed of talking and type of language.

Once you established that connection, begin to lead the client into a different space, generally what hypnotists call a trance or downtime, where the person is encouraged to explore his inner world. (In NLP terms, uptime is when your senses are focused on the outside world, while downtime is related to your inner thoughts.)

So, to pace a respondent, begin by matching her postures and gestures, choice of verbs, tone of voice, etc. Once the connection is made, you can change the tempo and sensory system to elicit responses from all senses — e.g., what did you see, hear, feel, smell, taste or think?

Write down your own examples here:

....
....
....
....
....
....
....
....

For example,
How are you doing?

Don't just say fine! Instead say *"I'm doing fine/well."*

This connects better because the person asking the question used the word "**doing**"

Always...well, not always, but try to use previous words, adjectives of the person you're speaking to. it helps to build rapport.

Additional learning:
Intelligent Personal Branding Intro

Using subliminal messaging:
(Derren Brown)

BRAND MARKET.

In order to discover your market, you need to ask yourself and answer some important questions.

Questions like;

Question 1: Who wants your product now?

You must discover those who really need your product or service URGENTLY or by necessity. This will let you know those who already have the desire for the solution you are providing or those who already feel the pain of not having the kind of product or service that you provide.

To these kinds of people, money could not be an issue because the intensity of their desire or pain would make them see the value of the product beyond the amount of money involved in getting it.

Make sure that you always have these kinds of people as your clients, they will keep the cash flow for your business.

Question 2: Who's interested?

The next kind of people are the people who are genuinely interested in your product and solutions but they are also mindful about the pricing. So, for these kinds of people, you need to amplify the value of your product and make them connect emotionally with the product, this should blur the lines of the money consciousness and amplify the sense of value consciousness of the product.

When you are engaging these people, you must learn to ask intelligent questions that allow you to know **why they are interested**. Once you find the core reason for their interest, then you must engage NLP techniques to keep them engaged and curious.

Register the words they use in describing their interest and the adjectives and the feelings associated with their means of communication.

For example;
If the customers say; *"I want a fantastic service from you"*, you do not say *"That's great! We can do that for you."*

That would not connect well with the customer you must mirror their words. So, you would say;

"Fantastic! We would be pleased to give you an experience."

And remember, it's not just words you speak, you must make it emotional and be truthful with your comments. Don't fake it. Customers can sense when you are not being truthful or if all you are worried about it to make the sale. Let them know that you really care about their wellbeing and interests.

Question 3: Who's not interested?
In as much as you think you do not need those who are not interested, there is a lot you can learn from them and with the right entry, connection and persuasion, they could become loyal customers in future.

This is also a good test for you. As a brand, you should not be satisfied only with those who like and are interested in your brand. You need to know why people do not like or have no interest in your brand as well. This will help you to make the necessary adjustments to your brand in the future especially if you are thinking of growing your brand and want it to reach more people.

One of the questions you need to ask them is **why aren't they interested** and the next question should be **why should they be interested**.

Notice their choice of words and the feelings associated with every word and feedback you get. You will need them when you have to develop your brand product and engage other markets.

Question 4: Who will never be interested?
No matter how good, excellent or persuasive your message or brand product is, there are people who would not be interested.

Note that *there is a difference between someone needing something and someone being interested in that thing.*
Something can actually be very useful, valuable or needful to a person but they are not interested. This may be as a result of various reasons. It could be that there is a knowledge gap that the person is intentionally doing nothing about and not interested in doing anything about.

The person may not desire the technology needed to do such a task. The person may be happy delegating the responsibility to another person. The person could just be traditional and do not seek change of any kind right now or in the future.

You can have these people at arm's length, once in a while (a long while), you can reach out to them to see if anything has changed with them. There is power in consistency but you must make sure that for these kinds of people, your consistency doesn't become irritating.

Remember, always take into account how people feel about your brand. Ensure that you keep them within the range of **excited, happy, satisfied, interested and curious**

Question 5: Who I don't want to be interested? (Brand protection)

In as much as you want your product to reach as many people as possible, depending on the message of your brand and the aura you want around it (perception), there are some kinds of people you would not want to be associated with your brand especially if some of the things that matter to you are qualities like; success, class, premium, etc.

It is your duty to protect the image and perception of your brand. If the wrong kinds of people are seen to patronize you frequently, it could prevent the right kinds of people from paying attention to your brand.

CONCLUSION

Branding will keep evolving with time. As the needs of people change and the means through which communication is done changes as well as the flexible patterns of modern meaning and implications.

When it comes to financial engagements, blockchain is the latest technology and to this end, you must make sure that your brand communication and commerce is blockchain friendly. The quicker you are able to do that, the better for you.

Blockchain, Artificial Intelligence, Virtual and Mixed Realities would be the new perception dictation of the trend of industries, and to this you must make sure that you have a good representation of your brand to project your visibility and communicate your brand core message and ideologies.

Human interaction would still be needful, that means you will need to find more convincing, persuasive means to communicate and make sure that you have a front row seat in the heads and minds of the market.

I wish you all the best.

Cheers,
'Harkheindzel' Kenny Omiyale
harkheindzelkenny@gmail.com
+2348182593790
Lagos, Nigeria

Additional information:
What is branding
Emotional storytelling